CW00499224

MATCHBOX TOYS

Nick Jones

Published in Great Britain in 2016 by Shire Publications Ltd (part of Bloomsbury Publishing Plc), PO Box 883, Oxford, OX1 9PL, UK.

1385 Broadway, 5th Floor New York, NY 10018, USA.

E-mail: shire@shirebooks.co.uk
www.shirebooks.co.uk

A CIP catalogue record for this book is available from the British Library.

Shire Library no. 826.   ISBN-13: 978 1 78442 038 3

PDF e-book ISBN: 978 1 78442 184 7

ePub ISBN: 978 1 78442 183 0

Nick Jones has asserted his right under the Copyright, Designs and Patents Act, 1988, to be identified as the author of this book.

Typeset in Adobe Garamond Pro and Gill Sans

Printed in China through World Print Ltd.

16 17 18 19 20   10 9 8 7 6 5 4 3 2 1

COVER IMAGE
Cover design and photography by Peter Ashley, featuring a Moko Lesney Matchbox Series toy of a Bedford Evening News van. Back cover: Matchbox Collector badge, Peter Ashley collection.

TITLE PAGE IMAGE
The Esso Sales and Service Station MG-1c dates from 1961. It is shown with the Esso Petrol Pumps and Sign A1a, Lomas Ambulance 14c, Routemaster Bus 5d, Ford Anglia 7b, Ford Zodiac 33a towing the Bluebird Dauphine caravan 23c, and the Major Pack Bedford Tractor and York Trailer M-2. Inside the showroom are the Vauxhall Victor Estate 38b and Ford Thames Estate Car 70a.

CONTENTS PAGE IMAGE
The BP Motorway Service Station and Forecourt MG-1f dates from 1969. It is shown here with the Mercedes 'Binz' Ambulance 3c, Mercedes 300se 46c, Lamborghini Marzal 20d, BMC Pininfarina 56c, MG 1000 64b and Dodge StakeTruck 4d. Inside the showroom are the Volkswagen 1600TL 67b, Field Car 18e and Alfa (Romeo) Carabo 75c.

DEDICATION
For the members of the Vintage British Diecast Forum, who encouraged me to write this book and have assisted me in the task.

ACKNOWLEDGEMENTS
The author would like to thank all the collectors, enthusiasts and friends who have provided him with information and checked details, especially Hugh Stiles, Joe P. Allen, Mick Bruce, George Marshal, Antonin Schenk, Mick Flack, Alex Lavery, the members of the Vintage British Diecast Forum, and the very helpful staff at Shire Publications. He is also grateful to Steve Barfield for the loan of photographs from his collection at www.regularwheel.com; to Gary Galvin and Numeshree Pillay for making their collections available to photograph; to George Marshal, who supplied photographs; and to www. vectis.co.uk for the loan of photographs.

A NOTE ON MODEL NUMBERING
Models produced in the 1-75 series never exceeded the number 75, but would begin the sequence again at 1 with a suffix of the next letter of the alphabet. Hence, the first 75 models were 1a to 75a; the second 75 models were 1b to 75b, and soforth.

Shire Publications supports the Woodland Trust, the UK's leading woodland conservation charity. Between 2014 and 2018 our donations are being spent on their Centenary Woods project in the UK.

CONTENTS

THE BIRTH OF LESNEY 1947–56

The Cement Mixer is usually found in green with orange or red wheels. Because it is usually found in one piece, it does not command very high prices.

Lesney Products Ltd was registered as a company on 19 January 1947 by two former schoolmates, Leslie Smith and Rodney Smith (unrelated), who had both served in the armed forces and used their military gratuity pay to purchase a die-casting machine from Rodney's pre-war employer, the Die Cast Machine Tools Company (DCMT). They had rented a derelict pub in Edmonton in north London called the Rifleman and set up their machinery in the saloon bar. The fledgling company was called 'Lesney', an amalgamation of 'Leslie' and 'Rodney', and 'Products', because they were not sure exactly what they would be making.

Their first order was for a diecast string-cutter, for which they had a local toolmaking company make the dies. As the toolmakers had also made themselves a copy of the dies, no further orders were forthcoming.

Shortly afterwards, another DCMT worker, John William Odell (usually known as Jack), approached them and asked about setting up his own die-casting machine in the Rifleman. He had originally set up his ex-army die-casting machine at his council house but the council had ordered him to remove it or face eviction. This turned out to be very fortunate for all concerned because Jack was an experienced toolmaker

and a natural engineer. Jack already had his first order for ten thousand ceiling hooks, so Jack became a partner in the company. Jack made the tools, Rodney did the die-casting, and Leslie did the accounts and sales.

Towards Christmas 1947 new orders began to slow down, so they looked for something else to make and their attention turned to toys. They bought a Dinky Toys Aveling Barford road roller and made tools to produce a similar toy for about one-third of the price of the Dinky. The Aveling Barford became the first Lesney toy to be released. It never had a tinplate baseplate like the Dinky and the roof canopy supports were diecast, whereas on the Dinky they were wire. The Lesney Aveling Barford was an instant success, not only because it was at least as good as the Dinky but also because it was cheaper and, furthermore, it could be sold anywhere, unlike the Dinky version, which could be sold only by authorised retailers. This made it ideal for smaller toyshops and newsagents to stock.

It was soon followed by the Lesney portable Cement Mixer, which came about because one was spotted in use on a construction site near the Rifleman; at lunchtime they visited the site armed with a tape measure and notepad and measured up the mixer. It was made to a larger scale than the Aveling Barford but

The large-scale Road Roller. Green with red wheels is the most common colour. The very rare red, orange and tan examples can fetch high prices.

The Crawler Tractor is often confused with an almost identical one made by Benbros that, fortunately, does have the maker's name on the base.

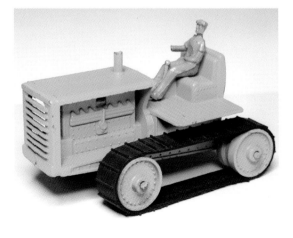

the finished model was about the same size, about 4 inches (100 mm).

Next came the Caterpillar Crawler Tractor, which went on sale in 1947–8. It was very loosely based on a Dinky Blaw Knox bulldozer but Lesney were gaining confidence in their own die-casting skills and produced a vehicle that was superior to the Dinky simply because it featured a fully detailed engine. About the time the Crawler was released, a Caterpillar Crawler Bulldozer version was also made available. Both the Tractor and the Bulldozer may be found with a separate light-brown diecast driver, but drivers are quite rare. The Bulldozer driver casting was very similar to the Prime Mover driver casting (see below).

The next toy was released in 1949: a firm favourite among toy collectors, it was the Horse-Drawn Milk Float. The Milk Float would have been a much more familiar vehicle to children than the previous toys, which were based on types confined to construction sites or road works, and so it was almost certainly a better seller. It was not only the first toy to feature hand-applied trim but also the first to be packed in its own box rather than in a retailer's box of six.

Also released in 1949 was the Horse-Drawn Rag and Bone Cart; it was not such a good seller as the Milk Float and so it is much harder to find. The horse and driver were the same as used on the Milk Float but the driver was painted a light brown. The front turntable and horse shafts were also as used on the Milk Float, but there the similarity ends. The set came with seven pieces of junk: a bicycle frame, a bucket, a toilet cistern, a

The Caterpillar Bulldozer sometimes has a driver, but more often not. Early examples have a blade-lifting handle attached to the front axle.

mangle handle, a bedstead and a tin bath, all of which were diecast and unpainted, plus a diecast wooden box that was painted brown. Like the Milk Float, the Rag and Bone Cart was packed in its own box but, despite this, many of the pieces of junk have been lost over the years and so to find a complete cart with all of its junk is extremely rare.

Also released in 1949 was the Soap Box Racer, which is probably more commonly known as a go-cart, a type of vehicle made by young boys that featured four old pram wheels fixed to a plank of wood and topped off with a wooden box for the rider to sit in. Although it was a well-executed model that included a highly detailed rider, it never sold in great numbers and so it is the rarest and most sought-after of all Lesney toys today. Although production figures were not kept, a figure of 144 units produced has been recorded, but many of these may have gone back into the smelting pot, and it is estimated that fewer than twenty Soap Box Racers probably survive in collections.

The Milk Float and the Rag and Bone Cart. The blue Milk Float is rare but the Rag and Bone Cart is almost impossible to find, especially in good condition.

The founders of Lesney Matchbox, Sir Jack Odell OBE and Sir Leslie Smith OBE. (Getty)

Consequently the Racer can command an extremely high price today.

By late 1949 Lesney had outgrown the Rifleman public house and so they moved a few miles south to a vacant factory in Shacklewell Lane, Hackney. The Rifleman was demolished soon after Lesney moved out. With the 1951 Festival of Britain being planned, Lesney decided to invest some of its profits into producing a Coronation Coach to celebrate the event, but before the Coach could be put into production the Korean War broke out and a ban was placed on using zinc for toy production, so the completed but unused dies were put into storage. Also at this time it was found that zinc, when in contact with the lime in plaster, would corrode and disintegrate, and so many of their contracts for household electrical fittings were cancelled. Lesney fell on hard times and Rodney Smith decided he wanted no further involvement with the company. He was paid £8,000 for his shares and left the story.

To get around the ban on making zinc-based toys, one of Lesney's distributors, Richard Kohnstam, trading as Moko, suggested that Lesney made a tinplate 'Jumbo the Elephant' similar to one that his family had been importing from Germany before the Second World War. Lesney did make the Elephant and it closely resembled the original German Jumbo made by Blomer & Schuler except that the legs were diecast instead of tinplate on the original. The lithographed design was also different and a woollen tail, bought from a local shop, was added, but the toy was very short-lived because the Korean War was going through a critical stage and the government completely banned the use of any zinc for toy production.

Meanwhile Lesney had endured the slump in business. They had plenty of zinc but few orders, so they tried their

hand at making components for the motor industry. This went rather well simply because their competitors were unable to purchase the zinc. Then in early 1952 King George VI died and three months later the Korean War ended. This meant that the ban on zinc for toy production would soon be over and a new queen would shortly be having her coronation. The Lesney Coronation Coach was a wonderful piece of die-casting. It was the largest toy that they had ever made, measuring an amazing 15 inches in length (370 mm), but Jack Odell wanted to make a smaller version and came up with the tiny 4.5-inch-long model, which was to decorate hundreds of thousands of celebratory cakes during the Coronation.

The large Coronation Coach was a heavy and robust piece of die-casting. The coach itself was made from Mazac (also known as Zamac), a mixture of 94 per cent zinc, 5 per cent aluminium and 1 per cent magnesium – standard stuff for Lesney.

Jumbo the Elephant, Muffin the Mule, the small Coronation Coach and the Conestoga Wagon. The small Coronation Coach sold a million pieces despite the horses having only two legs.

The Coach could be gold-painted, silver-plated or gold-plated, but the horses were made from slush-cast lead (where molten lead was poured into a mould and tipped out again so only a thin shell of lead remained), and for these Lesney turned to another local die-casting company, Benbros in neighbouring Walthamstow. Benbros had years of experience in the manufacture of slush-cast lead toys, and Lesney would not have lead in their factory as a pennyweight of lead could contaminate a hundredweight of Mazac, causing cracking and crumbling of castings. When the large Coronation Coach first went into production some eight hundred were made before someone realised that it contained both king and queen figures, while on the day of the Coronation the Queen would be travelling alone. So the dies had to be modified to remove the figure of the king, but the job was rushed so he was removed only from the knees upwards.

The small Coronation Coach was just 4.5 inches long (115 mm) and this version was completely diecast in Mazac. It was usually silver-plated, but a few silver-painted models exist, and sometimes the silver has tarnished and appears to be gold. The horses were spray-painted off-white, and additional detailing was applied by hand; the horses' blankets and the riders' jackets were painted red, the saddles were painted gold and the riders' hats and boots were painted black, so these were quite labour-intensive, but the completed item was remarkable. Some have 'England' cast on the coach but all have 'A Moko toy by Lesney made in England' cast along the horse drawbar. This is the first mention of 'Moko' on any Lesney toy and that is because Moko, a toy wholesaler, was given sole rights to market the small coach. Moko was to play a major role in the marketing of Lesney and later Matchbox toys over the years to come.

The large-scale Coronation Coach was a fairly basic die-casting but the painted detail to the horses was all hand-applied and very time-consuming.

The next release was the Prime Mover and Bulldozer set, which was loosely based on an ex-military Diamond T tank transporter prime mover and trailer paired up with one of Lesney's earlier Bulldozers. The Prime Mover was a heavy truck that was always painted orange, and the trailer is usually painted light blue but a few have been found in light brown. The Bulldozer is usually yellow with red wheels and dozer blade, but Bulldozers in all-over green or all-over orange have also been found. The Prime Mover and Bulldozer set was packaged in a substantial blue cardboard box with a lift-off lid and was very suitable as a Christmas or birthday present.

The BBC's television series *Watch with Mother* supplied the next subject to be modelled by Lesney. It was a diecast Muffin the Mule puppet based on Muffin, the star of the show, and was financed and marketed by the toy wholesaler Moko for the BBC and manufactured by Lesney. The puppet was suspended on four strings with diecast finger rings. Although this was Lesney's first television-related toy, and very successful, there was to be no repetition until the 1980s, when Gerry Anderson's *Thunderbirds* sets were released. Sadly, Muffin

The Prime Mover set usually has a blue trailer but a few have been found with light brown trailers. Trailers with the drawbar still attached are very rare.

The Massey Harris Tractor is probably the most impressive and certainly the largest vehicle modelled by Lesney. It not only had steering but working suspension too.

came to an abrupt end when his presenter, Annette Mills, died unexpectedly and the television show was cancelled.

The Massey Harris Farm Tractor became the first toy to be modelled since before the zinc ban, and what a wonderful toy it was, measuring 8 inches long (200 mm) and fitted with very realistic black rubber tyres. The box stated it was number 1 from the Lesney 'Major Scale' series.

Number 2 was planned to be the Euclid Quarry Truck but it never went into production, because the first four models of the 'Miniatures' or '1-75' series were released at the same time as the Massey Harris and were so successful that the smaller models had to be kept in production because there was such a huge demand for them. The sole surviving Euclid, which was in the care of a Japanese collector, was sold at auction in early 2010 for more than £10,000.

In 1955 Lesney released a Conestoga Wagon, a type of horse-drawn vehicle that was very familiar from western films. It was 5 inches long, including the six horses pulling it. It was packed into a full-colour box marked as 'No. 59' and priced at 59 cents. The majority of them were shipped to the United States and Canada. The Conestoga was sold in the United Kingdom but it is fairly rare there.

MATCHBOX

"MATCHBOX"
FARNBOROUGH • MEASHAM
CAR AUCTION COLLECTION
M-8   MAJOR PACK

MATCH
MODELS of YESTERYEAR
MAJOR
M-9
PACK

1965
"MATCHB
SERIES
the fastest sel
miniature sca
models in th
world!

THE '1-75' SERIES REGULAR WHEELS 1953–69

THE FIRST FOUR Miniatures or '1-75' series were released in 1953 and all were based on scaled-down models from the major-scale range. The story that has been related over the years was that Jack Odell's daughter Annie was told that she was allowed to take a toy to school only if it would fit inside a regular matchbox. But the truth is that she kept bringing home spiders and creepy-crawlies inside a matchbox, so Jack offered to make her a toy to fit inside the matchbox if she would promise not bring any more spiders home. Annie agreed and Jack made her a scaled-down brass Road Roller based on the large-scale model. Annie was delighted with her new toy and proudly took it to school with her. When the other children saw it they all wanted one, so Jack scaled down the dies from the major-scale Road Roller and put it into production.

The first models appeared in the shops just before Christmas. The initial response from shopkeepers was that they looked like 'cheap Christmas cracker trash' and they were very slow to sell, but after Christmas they began to sell faster than anyone could have dreamt simply because they could be bought with children's pocket money. The first four models were the Road Roller 1a, the Site Dumper 2a, the Cement Mixer 3a and the Massey Harris Tractor 4a – all construction or farm vehicles. But the next release in 1954 was a London Bus 5a, followed by the Euclid Quarry Truck 6a, Horse-Drawn Milk Float 7a and Caterpillar Tractor 8a,

Opposite:
Matchbox Series
Fred Bronner
Corporation
1965 Trade
Catalogue cover.
(Vectis)

The first three models from 1953. All were from the construction industry and would not have been familiar to younger children. The Road Roller was a scaled-down copy of the 1947 large-scale model and it can be found in three different shades of green.

The second 'enlarged' version of the Bedford Low Loader 28b has to be the hardest casting to find. It was in production for only two years and can be found in mid- or dark green with a light brown trailer. Early versions had metal wheels, later ones grey plastic wheels.

which would all have been more recognisable to younger children, and the range took off and never looked back.

In 1955 ten more models were introduced, including a Fire Engine 9a, an Esso Petrol Tanker 11a and a Daimler Ambulance 14a. The first release of the Esso Tanker was in green, then two different shades of yellow and finally red, but the green version is quite rare. Also the Prime Mover 15a was normally painted orange but the first release in yellow is very hard to find, especially in mint condition.

Ten brand-new models entered the range in 1956 and the Road Roller and London Bus were replaced by similar but slightly larger models. The range had so far been all commercial vehicles but the first motor-car proper was the MG Midget 19a. Although a Land Rover 12a had been made, it was

British heavy lorries: (rear) Guy Pickfords Van 46b; (front left) Tate & Lyle Tanker 10c; (front right) ERF Ever Ready Batteries Flatbed Truck 20b.

essentially a farm vehicle. The Berkeley Cavalier Caravan 23a in metallic green and the Bedford Low Loader 27a in two-tone blue are ones to look out for as both are very rare.

In 1957 fourteen new models were released and four replacements. By this time Lesney was exporting a large number of models to Germany and to the United States, so to keep the foreign customers interested they produced some models that would be more familiar to them. The American Ford Station Wagon 31a, the Volkswagen Van 34a and the Volkswagen 1200 25b were introduced for that purpose. The Ford Zodiac 33a in dark blue is the rarest one from that year but sun-faded dark green and dark blue-green models exist and are often mistaken for the rare one.

Eighteen new models and a further twelve slightly enlarged replacements arrived in 1958 and grey or black plastic wheels replaced the diecast metal wheels that had been used until now.

European saloon cars (left to right): Hillman Minx 43a; Vauxhall Cresta 22b; and Volkswagen 1200 25b. The Vauxhall can be found in several different colour schemes and for the collector it is probably the most desirable model made by Lesney.

The London Trolley Bus 56a is one of the few models that can be found with all four types of wheel: grey metal, grey, silver and black plastic. It usually has Peardrax decals but the final issue was fitted with Visco-Static decals that are normally found on the 5b Bus or more commonly the 5c Bus.

Military vehicles appeared for the first time with the introduction of the M3 Personnel Carrier 49a (US Halftrack), the Saracen Personnel Carrier 54a and the DUKW Amphibian 55a. The rarest models from this year were the Morris Minor 46a in light brown and the Vauxhall Victor 45a in red. The Morris Minor can also be found in blue but is more common in dark green. The Minor is generally difficult to find in any colour because a large quantity of them were stolen when the warehouse was broken into, and also because it was not in production for very long; it was not a good seller because it was a rather small model and the colour scheme of dark green did not help. It might have sold better if Lesney had recoloured the model and released it as a Police Panda Car. There had been a Fire Engine and an Ambulance in the range since 1955 but it was not until 1963 that a Police Car finally joined them.

Eight of the fifteen new models in 1959 were military, and seven models were deleted to be replaced with enlargements or new versions. The 'crimped' or squashed axle ends were updated to machine-burred rounded ends and it was decided to limit the range to seventy-five models. Now all new models

would be inserted into the range and given the number from a deleted model. (A very few Triumph T110 Motorcycles 4b have been found cast with the number 78 and are eagerly sought by collectors.) Thus the 'Matchbox Miniatures' became known as the '1-75' series. Wheels in silver plastic were fitted to selected models and the Ford Thunderbird 75a was the first model to have plastic windows fitted from the start of production.

In 1960 twelve new models were introduced, including the Cadillac Sixty Special 27c, the Ford Fairlane Station Wagon 31b and the Volkswagen 1200 25b. The Cadillac can be found in any of four metallic colours; lilac and silver grey

By 1962 there were eleven military vehicles in the range: Halftrack 49a, Saracen 54a, DUKW 55a, Scout Car 61a, 6x6 Army Truck 62a, Army Ambulance 63a, Army Wrecker 64a, Armoured Car 67a, Radio Truck 68a, Water Tanker 71a, and RAF Refueller 73a.

The Triumph T110 4c (rear); Harley Davidson 66b (front left); Lambretta TV175 36c (front right).

The early American cars (left to right): Cadillac 27c in silver or in metallic lilac; Pontiac Convertible 39b in yellow or metallic mauve; Chevrolet Impala 57b in metallic blue with a light blue roof.

An early presentation set. This is the Commercial Motors Gift Set PS-4, which dates from 1959 and was also released as the 'Lastwagen und Omnibuse' set for the German market.

are fairly common but brown and green are rare. The Ford can be found in yellow or green and pink; the yellow version is rare but is often confused with the earlier number 31a, which was always painted yellow. The Volkswagen Beetle 25b also has a few interesting variations to look out for. Flip open the engine cover; a black-painted engine is quite rare. Also check for the spelling on the base, which should read 'Volkswagen', but early versions have it misspelled as 'Volkswagon'. Very late issues were released with black plastic wheels but these are seldom seen and may have been available only in gift sets, which might explain the rarity of this variation.

Thirteen new models appeared in 1961. The Commer Milk Float 21c with its plastic milk crates became the first model to be made using plastic components (apart from the wheels), but the star of the year has to be the Bluebird Dauphine Caravan 23c, which can be found in all-over metallic green or in metallic lilac with a crimson baseplate and a black door; both variations are very rare. The Dauphine was originally intended to be made with windows but these were omitted at the last minute. However, a few models, in both metallic green and metallic lilac, are known to exist fitted with windows with or without a cross-hatching pattern engraved into them. These are extremely rare and fetch a very high price when one does

come up for sale. The final version in metallic lilac with black plastic wheels is also quite rare, so there are plenty of gems to look out for when it comes to caravans.

Twelve new models were introduced in 1962. The Pontiac Convertible 39b was the first to be fitted with a plastic interior, and Pontiacs painted metallic violet are particularly sought-after by American collectors as seemingly only the fairly common yellow versions were exported to the United States. The Jaguar E Type 32b can be found in dark or light metallic red and shades can vary considerably but one rare variation is painted metallic bronze. To be sure you have the bronze version, check the underside, as sun-faded light metallic red

Matchbox toys can be subject to fading when left in direct sunlight. These two Austin Cambridges 29b were the exact same colour when they were made.

The Morris J2 Pick-up 60a was always painted blue and carried decals for the 'Builders Supply Company' but 'Supply Company' can be found in black or white ink and the cab can be found with or without a rear window. Shown are the grey, silver and black plastic-wheeled versions.

can easily be mistaken for the rare bronze. The underside is not usually affected by sunlight and should still be in the colour it was intended to be.

Only ten new models were made in 1963. The Ford Fairlane Police Car 55b and the Ford Fairlane Fire Chief 59b used the same basic casting but with different paint colours and decals. Both are quite rare to find with silver or grey plastic wheels although grey-wheeled Fire Chiefs are a little more common. Either model can be found fitted with the baseplate from the other, but these are not common. One Police Car that has the white roof dome light from the Fire Chief instead of the usual blue version has been found but it is not clear if this is simply an error piece or a little-known variation.

Also from this year was the Mercedes Benz 220SE 53b, which was the first miniature to be modelled with opening doors. It can be found in maroon or dark red and with grey, silver or black wheels.

There were ten new models in 1964. The new Bedford BP Petrol Tanker 25c in white, green and yellow was also recoloured to white and blue and fitted with Aral decals for the European market. The Jaguar Mk10 28c has some interesting variations. The first release did not have 'Matchbox Series' on the base and was fitted with grey wheels; all later issues had the base modified to include 'Matchbox Series' and were fitted with black wheels. The early issue is extremely rare. The Snow Trac 35b was originally intended to have three windows on the back, but when it was released it had only a single rear window. The search is on for a possible three-window variant.

The Volkswagen-based Snow-Trac 35b. The first version had Snow-Trac decals. The second one had no decals and smooth sides, and the final version had 'Snow-Trac' cast into the sides. Although a few Snow-Tracs have been found with grey tracks they are thought not to be original.

Sixteen new models were introduced in 1965. Early releases of both the Trailer Caravan 23d and the Chevrolet Taxi 20c can be found with grey wheels, and both are very rare. The Faun Crane Truck 30c, which is normally green and orange, has been discovered packed into a few gift sets painted turquoise and orange, which is also very rare, but what is possibly the most sought-after model in the range is the BP Dodge Wreck Truck 13d in the early colour scheme of green cab with yellow back. BP was paying Lesney to promote its company and did not like the colours, so they were reversed to yellow cab with green back. Models with the early colour scheme are extremely rare and highly valuable.

An assortment of Boats and Trailers. The second one made, 48b, can be found in white, cream or red plastic, and the motor can be found in a silver- or gold-plated finish. The Cabin Cruiser 9d was made for over twenty-five years, continuing well into the Superfast era.

Late-issue American cars. The Mercury Station Wagon 73c is fairly common but the Chevrolet Taxi 20c with grey wheels and the Lincoln Continental 31c in metallic lime green are both extremely rare.

Twenty new models were added in 1966, including the best-selling model of all time, the Ford GT40 41c. It was normally off-white with yellow hubs but was recoloured for the G-4 gift set to yellow with yellow hubs. One hard-to-find version was off-white with red hubs, but the most elusive variant is the pre-production model fitted with wire wheels. It was thought by many collectors to be a fake or a custom (where a model has been altered from its original condition by a previous owner) but close examination of photographs

A regular-wheel G-6 Truck set that dates from 1966. A few G-6 sets have been found to contain a Crane Truck 30c in turquoise rather than the usual green.

The bestselling Ford GT40 41c was first made with regular wheels, and later with Superfast wheels. It is normally painted white or bronze but this yellow version was recoloured especially for the Race 'n' Rally G-4 gift set.

in early Matchbox publications has shown it to be genuine. The Opel Diplomat 36c was painted gold but, like the Faun Crane, has been found recoloured to turquoise and packed into gift sets.

There were thirteen new models in 1967. Surprisingly, there were no real rarities made that year although some examples of one of the commonest models, the Claas Combine Harvester 65c, can be found without the hole in the baseplate that was actually a spindle hole used during the painting process, and on other examples the bottom rung of the ladder that hung below the bodywork was cast open. The open rung often bent during assembly, so it was soon filled in. Harvesters with either or both of these variations are very hard to find.

Nineteen new models were released in 1968. Again, no real rarities were made that year, except for one much sought-after model. The Mercury Cougar 62c is normally metallic green with a red interior, but a few of these painted in cream gloss with white interior have been found in South Africa and New Zealand. Also, these early pre-production pieces do not have a rear-view mirror moulded into the windscreen as found on the standard model.

Only seven new models were introduced in 1969 and development of new models was put on hold halfway through

Overleaf: A worker fitting the tyres to toy trucks on the assembly line at the Lesney factory in Hackney, London, 17 June 1968. (Getty)

Workers checking the quality of finished toys on the assembly line, 17 June 1968. (Getty)

the year. This was because Mattel's brand-new 'Hot Wheels' range with low-friction wheels, high-speed axles and bright paintwork had been launched and Matchbox's sales figures had plummeted to an unprecedented degree. But Mattel had made a serious error in that they did not patent the new

The British-made Matchbox display unit. Unlike the Bronner displays made in the United States, which were redesigned yearly, this one was kept in production for many years, but it is nevertheless very rare and highly collectable.

Designers with the latest in the Matchbox series of die-cast model cars at the Lesney factory, 17 June 1968. (Getty)

axles and so Lesney's Matchbox plant set about converting its entire range to the new 'Speedwheels' as quickly as possible.

Also at this time it was decided to liven up the range with much brighter colours in order to compete with the new Hot Wheels Spectraflame mirror-like finish. As a result many of the new Superfast coloured bodies found their way on to baseplates with the older-type wheels, and vice-versa, giving us the crossover pieces of the transitional era that are among the most sought-after models today.

THE '1-75' SERIES SUPERFAST ISSUES 1969–83

CONVERTING TO THE new Superfast wheels with their thinner, low-friction axles meant that Lesney had to adapt to making the new wheel sets. This was where the wheels were fitted to the axle before installing them on the car, so it also meant that each model would need to have a unique plastic axle carrier fitted inside the base, and the diecast base needed to be enlarged to make room for the axle carrier. On the few models that were not suitable to have axle carriers installed a wheel set was fitted into a small axle clip that was inserted into the bottom of the baseplate. Whichever method was used, a great deal of retooling was necessary for the entire range.

The Ferrari Berlinetta 75b was usually painted green during the regular-wheels era and red in the Superfast era. Transitional models exist, either regular-wheels models fitted with red bodies or green bodies fitted with Superfast wheels. Both are very desirable.

The ever popular Volkswagen Camper 23e was first painted blue, and later issues were painted orange. The blue version with a petrol filler flap cast into the side is quite hard to find. The filler flap was deleted early on to allow for the placement of stickers, but stickers were never fitted to the blue model.

As well as the redesigning of the wheels, axles, axle carriers and baseplates, the colour schemes were brightened up as well, and where it was possible for the regular-wheel and Superfast components to be interchanged then they were. After all, Lesney was only making children's toys, so it did not matter if a Superfast model had a regular-wheel colour – which gives us the models that are so sought after by present-day collectors. There were few regular-wheel models that appeared in Superfast colours, except for the Land Rover Safari 12c in metallic gold, the Mustang 8e in red gloss, the Lincoln Continental 31c in metallic lime green, the

All three trucks, the Dodge Stake Truck 4d, Leyland Petrol Tanker 32c and Dodge Dumper Truck 48c, were carried over from the regular-wheel era. The Petrol Tanker and Stake Truck colours were unaltered but the Dumper was recoloured to yellow and blue.

Volkswagen 1600TL 67b in metallic purple and the Ferrari Berlinetta 75b in red gloss, but the Superfasts were a different story. The most desirable have to be the Pontiac GP Coupe 22c in red gloss, the Lincoln Continental 31c in sea-green gloss and the Ford Zodiac 53c in metallic light blue.

However, many fakes have been made over the years and are still being made today, particularly the Land Rover 12c in blue gloss and the Ferrari Berlinetta 75b in metallic green, where a standard green regular-wheel Ferrari and a Superfast Ferrari in red can easily be converted into two valuable models by switching the baseplates, so extreme caution should be taken when purchasing any of these transitional models.

Some models were deleted soon after they were converted to Superfast, such as the Land Rover Fire Engine 57c, which is quite rare, and even harder to find complete with the original box. Others had major modifications and recolours, such as the Mercury Cougar 62c in light metallic green, which had

The big American saloons were also carried over from the regular-wheel era.

The Mercury Cougar 'Rat Rod' 62d in light green or lime green was an attractive model but the Hot Rod Draguar 36d and the Road Dragster 19e were perhaps a little too unrealistic.

Although the Mercedes Truck 1d and its Trailer 2e appeared in only one colour, the Superfast version was recoloured several times. In addition to those shown here, it can be found in metallic gold, military olive green and military olive drab.

an opening cut into the bonnet and a large chrome engine fitted; its rear wheel wells were enlarged and a pair of larger wheels fitted to give it the dragster look. It was also recoloured to light yellow gloss or light green gloss.

The Mustang 8e was briefly released in the regular-wheel colour of white with a red interior; it was then recoloured to red and later to orange-red with either a red or a white interior. Finally it was given the dragster look with big wheels and exposed engine, giving us the Wildcat Dragster 8f. A few models were not converted to Superfast but kept their regular wheels, such as the Alvis Stalwart 61b, the Claas Combine Harvester 65c and the Ford Tractor 39c and its Hay Trailer 40c; and of course the Case Bulldozer 16d kept its rubber tracks.

One model that was deleted probably much too soon was the Pontiac GP Coupe 22c. It first appeared in the regular-wheel colour of red gloss and it was immediately recoloured to metallic purple, only to be replaced by the Freeman Inter-City Commuter 22d shortly after. The metallic purple is quite rare but can be found, but very few of the red-gloss version are known to exist. It is probably the most desirable Superfast model, not just because it is so rare but because it was such a beautiful design.

The 'transitional' era began in mid-1969 during the final days of the regular-wheeled models and extended into the first year or two of the Superfast era. During this period models might be made with components from both the regular-wheel

There were four basic colours for the Rolls Royce Silver Shadow 69c – metallic blue, metallic light gold, metallic gold, and metallic lime gold – but a few very desirable pre-production models have been found painted yellow gloss.

era and the Superfast era mixed together, but this usually meant that it was either a regular-wheeled model with the body in Superfast colours, or, more commonly, a Superfast model with a body in regular-wheel colours, although neither is particularly common.

The Setra Coach 12d is fairly common painted metallic gold but it can also be found in yellow gloss, metallic crimson and metallic purple. Green-tinted or clear plastic windows and a grey or white roof add to the variations available.

In 1970 Matchbox belatedly made a model of that British icon the Mini. The Racing Mini 29d was first released in metallic bronze, followed by orange gloss, and then red gloss. The red version with the racing number 3 sticker seems to be the hardest one to find.

Superfast models worth looking out for include the Ford Cortina 25d in metallic brown, the Faun Eight-Wheeled Crane 30c in red gloss with orange gloss crane boom, the Iron Fairy Crane 42c in an orangy-red gloss with a yellow gloss crane boom, the Refrigerator Truck 44c with a red gloss cab and turquoise gloss box, the Mercedes Benz 300SE 46c in metallic blue, the Ford Zodiac 53c in light metallic blue, the Morris 1100 64b in green gloss, and the Volkswagen 1600TL 67b in red gloss. There are a few other more common transitionals but these are the ones that are most sought after.

The Lamborghini Miura 33c can be found in the Superfast colour of gold with regular wheels and also in regular-wheels yellow fitted with Superfast wheels; both types can be found with a towing hitch cast into the front of the baseplate, but these are quite rare. There is also a bronze version with red seats that is fairly rare, and rarer still are yellow Miuras with white interior.

In 1970 Lesney at last released a Mini, the Racing Mini 29d. Originally intended to have the door handles, hinges and door outline cast in, it eventually went on sale with these details omitted so that it could be fitted with large stickers along the sides. However, a few were released with the door detailing and are eagerly sought by collectors. The standard colours for this model were metallic bronze, orange gloss or red gloss, but colour trials are known to exist in metallic gold or light blue gloss (a Swedish promotional).

The Formula I Racing Car 34f can be painted metallic dark pink, metallic blue, orange gloss or yellow gloss. The metallic blue is the hardest to find because it was available only in the Team Matchbox Superfast Champions G-4 gift set.

Ten models were not converted to Superfast, the reason usually given for this being that they were unsuitable for conversion, but many of the full-size vehicles were no longer being built and so the models were being phased out anyway. Another from the same year was the Ford Group 6 45c and the first release was in green gloss, which is very rare. Also in 1970 the Dodge Charger Mk III 52c joined the range. It was based on a futuristic prototype that never went into production but it showed in what direction the range was heading.

In 1971 the range shifted more towards the outlandish hot-rods and prototypes. The Dodge Dragster 70c was a prime example, with its lift-up Funny Car body and chromed V8 engine. Although it was always painted light or dark pink, there are at least seven different base colours, and more if the shades are counted. The Road Dragster 19e, Freeman Inter-City Commuter 22d and Alfa (Romeo) Carabo 75c also made it into the range, increasing the numbers of prototype and show cars, and it would be only a few years until there were hardly any normal road cars left. The following year saw the introduction of the Gruesome Twosome 4d, the Volks-Dragon 31d, the Vauxhall Guildsman 40d, the Blue Shark 61c and the Slingshot Dragster 64c; these were all fantasy cars that were never made.

Although the various beach buggies, hot Volkswagens and custom cars were popular, the inclusion of Italian supercars, show cars, prototypes and fantasy cars that were rarely if ever seen on the roads meant that for the most part they would not be recognisable to children. Gone were the days when you could buy a Matchbox model of Dad's car.

Introduced in 1973 were the 'Rolamatics', a small group of models with additional features that were intended to increase play value. These were operated by a peg on one of the wheels that when pushed along would turn a cam and drive each of the model's special features. Among them was the Piston Popper 10e, which had the top of the engine moulded in clear plastic and was fitted with red plastic pistons that would bounce up and down as the car was pushed. It was normally painted blue or yellow but one issue was produced in white specifically for the German market and is quite rare to find today. Another unusual Rolamatic was the Turbo Fury 69d, which had large fans sticking out of the back that would revolve as it was pushed along. The model was always painted red but is quite rare when found with scorpion decals. The Weasel 73d was an armoured car with a revolving turret that was painted in various shades of green, but the bronze version is quite rare.

By 1975 the '1-75' series consisted of only five normal road-going cars, but it was a turning point as the number of fantasy cars began to decline, being replaced with normal

road-going cars. Admittedly these were 'hotted up' with 'go faster' stripes and the like but they were models of actual cars that could be seen on the road every day. Fortunately most of the commercial vehicles still represented actual vehicles. The Daimler 'Londoner' Bus 17e, which was first made in 1972, had appeared in various colours with either 'Carnaby Street', 'Berger Paints' or 'Esso Extra Petrol' labels, but can also be found with 'Baron of Beef' labels, one of three different 'Sellotape' labels, 'Interchemicals and Plastics', 'Ilford HP5 Film', 'Eduscho Kaffee' or 'Borregaard Paper' labels, all of which are hard to find and fetch a premium over the standard Berger issues.

The majority of high-value pieces are the earlier transitionals but a few later issues, made after 1975, are sought after. The two chopper trikes, the Stingeroo 38d and the Chop Suey 49c with chromed forks, are both very rare. The Tow Joe Wrecker 74c is usually found in green or yellow but also occurs in red, which is hard to find, and also in yellow with 'Hitch Hiker' labels. Another wrecker, the Ford Heavy Wrecker 71c, is quite common in red and white with 'Esso' labels, but the dark blue version that did not have labels is rather rare. Another very hard-to-find model is the Sambron Jacklift 48e. The first release, possibly consisting of surplus promotional models, has the name 'Sambron' printed on the sides. The name was quickly deleted, so the named versions have become quite sought after.

The Dragon Wheels 43d and the Dodge Dragster 70c were both based on Funny Car dragsters with flip-up bodies and blown V8 engines. The Dragon Wheels was available only in two shades of green. The Dodge was available in pink or yellow, but with a variety of base colours and stickers.

This is a 'Rolamatic' model, one of several made whose play value Lesney tried to enhance with added features. Push the Piston Popper 10e and the pistons would go up and down. It was powered by a peg on the inside of the front wheel.

Some Superfast components were shipped to Brazil, where they were painted and assembled; these usually have a 'Roly Toys' label stuck to the base, but after several decades quite often the labels will have come off. Brazilian issues are usually painted in unusual colours that are not normally seen on British Matchbox toys. Likewise, Hungary and Bulgaria also had their own Matchbox cars. These were made using British dies but the bodies were cast, painted and assembled overseas and have the country of manufacture embossed on the base. Hungarian and Bulgarian models were also painted in a wide variety of colours and may well have non-standard interior colours. Bulgaria also chrome-plated and metal-coated various models.

Japan also had its own range of Superfast models. These used British baseplates and normally came in the standard colours, but they were always packed into boxes with Japanese script, which were not generally available outside Japan.

The Brazilian issues are quite rare and not seen much outside South America. The Hungarian and Bulgarian issues are generally available and do not usually command much of a premium. Some of the Japanese issues were re-imported back to the United Kingdom by collectors and dealers, so are generally available with their Japanese boxes, but these do fetch a moderate premium over standard models.

ACCESSORY PACKS, MAJOR PACKS AND THE KINGSIZE RANGE

BY 1956 THE miniatures or '1-75' series had grown into Lesney's best-selling range of toys and they wanted to build upon that success. This was done by introducing a collection of small-scale toys that were too large to fit into the standard-size Matchbox, yet still looked right when sat next to the miniatures. At this time the early large-scale toys were all taken out of production and the Accessory packs and the Major packs were launched. All bar one of the Accessory packs were not vehicles and they included Esso A-1a or BP A-1b Petrol Pumps and Sign, a Garage A-3a, a set of eight Road Signs A-4a and a Shop A-5a. The one vehicle that was included in the Accessory packs range was the Bedford Articulated Car Transporter A-2a, which is usually found in blue, but just before the model was deleted it was recoloured to red and grey, which is hard to find. There were variants fitted with metal wheels, grey and later black plastic wheels and enhanced with

Accessory pack A-1a, Esso Petrol Pumps and Sign, from 1957 and the A-1b BP Petrol Pumps and Sign that replaced it in 1963. The Esso set is fairly common but the BP set is slightly rarer, especially if it still has the plastic attendant, light stands and the box.

The Bedford Car Transporter A-2a was first made in 1957. On the top deck at the rear is the Ford Station Wagon 31b and in front the Jaguar 3.8 litre 65b. On the lower deck at the rear is the Ford Prefect 30a and in front the Cadillac Sixty Special 27c.

several different decals, so a complete line-up of this model's different variations takes up a lot of shelf space.

The Car Transporter A-2a would perhaps have been better suited to the Major pack range, which followed a few months later in early 1957. The Major packs were a collection of larger small-scale toys that were mostly trucks, but include a Ruston Bucyrus Power Shovel M-4a and a Massey Ferguson Combine Harvester M-5a. Two particular models were extremely popular: the Pickfords Scammell 200-Ton Transporter M-6a, which first appeared in maroon and dark blue, and later in dark red and blue, was a splendid model; likewise, the Hendrickson Double Freighter M-9a, which is probably better known as the 'Cooper Jarrett' because it was in that company's livery. It was released with a blue tractor unit with silver trailers displaying yellow 'Cooper Jarrett' decals, but one quite rare version has orange decals and another hard-

A Major pack Massey Ferguson 780 Combine Harvester M-5a that dates from 1959 can have a variety of wheel types and either a metal or plastic steering wheel. The rarest version has yellow plastic hubs front and rear and the version with orange hubs front and rear is almost as rare.

to-find version has grey trailers. Another one to look out for is the Guy Warrior Car Transporter M-8b, which normally had a turquoise tractor unit and an orange trailer, but small numbers of pre-production examples in all-over turquoise appear to have been sold in normal retail outlets. In 1967 the Major packs range was deleted and the models deemed suitable were moved into the Kingsize range.

The Kingsize range of models at first comprised mostly construction vehicles that were made to fit in with the then current Dinky and Corgi toys, which were made to a larger scale than Matchbox toys – not that Lesney ever kept to a particular scale for any of their models. Most of the range is generally available and there are few rarities but there are one or two worth looking out for. Among them is the Guy Warrior Car Transporter K-8 (formerly M-8), which kept its original Major pack colour scheme of turquoise and orange but was later recoloured to all-over yellow. During the recolour a few were issued with turquoise cabs and yellow trailers. Later another car transporter was released. This was the Daf K-11, which had a blue cab with a gold trailer. It was

Everyone's childhood favourite, the Hendrickson Interstate Double Freighter M-9a was a wonderful model with great play value. It is normally found with silver trailers and yellow 'Cooper Jarrett' decals. Grey trailers are hard to find, as are silver trailers with orange decals.

The Thames Trader and Jennings Cattle Truck M-7a joined the range in 1960. The pre-production version in light blue with a metallic copper trailer is extremely rare and even a play-worn example can be worth more than £1,000.

The 'Freuhof' Hopper Train M-4b from 1965 was a lovely model but it might have been a better seller if it had been made to a slightly smaller scale as it did not fit in with the 1-75 models being produced at that date. It has no significant variations. In 1967 it was moved into the Kingsize range as the new K-4b.

later recoloured to yellow and orange, but pre-production examples have been found in blue with a silver trailer.

It was not until K-21 was released that the first car made it into the range. This was the Mercury Cougar, which was painted gold and had red seats, but it is also available with white seats and this variation is quite rare. The next car, the Dodge Charger K-22, was painted metallic blue with a blue interior, but this one can also be found with a pre-production yellow interior, which is very rare. The next two cars were the Mercury Commuter Police Car K-23 and the Lamborghini Miura K-24, which were both copied from existing models in the '1-75' series.

In 1970, at the time when the '1-75' series was being converted to Superfast wheels, there was much disagreement among the Lesney management as to whether the Kingsize range should follow suit. Jack Odell wanted to keep the Kingsize range as it was but he was outvoted by the other company directors and so the Kingsize models were fitted with Superfast-type wheels and renamed 'Superkings'. But, given the choice, most collectors would have agreed with Jack Odell. There were never any track sets with their loops and high-speed curves made for the Superkings and among collectors it is generally thought that converting the whole range was a total waste of effort. Instead of increasing sales, it probably had the opposite effect. These larger-scale models were not aimed at children but more towards the older teenage collector, and the fitment of Superfast wheels must have made quite a few

The Speedkings Dodge Dragster K-22 from 1971 and the 'Bazooka' K-44 from 1973 were supposed to compete with the Dinky and Corgi ranges of the day. Although they were fairly well made they were never great sellers and so are relatively scarce, but they are not widely collected today.

of these older collectors lose interest. Whoever thought that fitting Speedwheels to construction vehicles would lead to increased sales was sadly mistaken.

Like the miniatures, many of the Superkings were revamped with brighter colours and a few were also given 'go-faster' stripes but on the whole the range was still heavily weighted towards construction, farm and heavy-haulage type vehicles. Eventually the range was split into two: the Superkings would keep the commercial vehicles, and the new range of Speedkings would be made up of cars. By 1974 a third range was added – the Battlekings, which were mostly army tanks and military vehicles, and a fourth range, the Seakings, comprising naval warships, followed by 1976.

Three models released into the Superkings range are of especial interest. The Dodge Twin Tipper K-16 was originally issued in green with yellow tippers and fitted with regular wheels. It was recoloured to yellow with blue tippers and at the same time it got Superfast wheels. The model was deleted shortly after, so the blue and yellow issue is fairly hard to find. It was replaced by the Ford LTS Tanker K-16b, which is seen with a variety of liveries, but the BP version is quite hard to find. Finally, the Bridgelayer K-44 was a wonderful toy with lots of play value, and it was also the biggest toy to appear in the Superkings range.

The Scammell Prime Mover and Trailer with Crawler Tractor K-8. The trailer normally has just the name 'Laing' on the sides but the early issue has a much longer decal with 'Civil Engineering Contractor' as well. (Vectis)

THE MODELS OF YESTERYEAR

The 'Models of Yesteryear' (MoY) range was launched in 1956. It was the brainchild of Jack Odell, who had a passion for vintage trucks, buses and steam vehicles. The range was aimed at adult collectors rather than children and so should have been kept to a set scale, but at least there was a little more use of colour in later years. The range was originally limited to sixteen vehicles but in 1975 the Hispano Suiza Y-17 broke this rule and by 1983, when Lesney was

These early steam vehicles date from the mid- to late 1950s. The Sentinel Steam Wagon Y-4 is harder to find with black plastic wheels and the Allchin Y-1 (misspelled 'Alchin' on the box) is very rare if fitted with the smooth rear wheels from the Y11, but many fakes exist.

declared bankrupt and manufacturing in Britain came to an end, the range stood at twenty-five models.

The earliest models are undoubtedly the most sought-after, particularly the 1924 Fowler Showman's Engine Y-9. It was originally intended to be part of the early large-scale series but owing to the success of the '1– 75' series it was never put into production. Instead, it was scaled down and moved into the Yesteryear range and sold at a premium of 4s 11d (the rest were sold at 2s 3d or 2s 6d), because of the large number of parts and the quantity of decals needed to decorate the model. It was painted dark maroon, maroon or red, but one much sought-after run was produced in purple.

Another interesting model was the Shand Mason Fire Engine Y-4b, a horse-drawn vehicle that first appeared with light grey horses, which were recoloured to white, then to dark bronze and finally to black. Early issues had 'Kent Fire Brigade' decals but these were changed for 'London Fire Brigade'. The grey horses version is very rare and the bronze horses version is rare.

Most of the bright components on this 1912 Packard Landaulet Y-11b, with the exception of the brake lever, were unintentionally not brass-plated. This is what collectors call an error piece.

The extremely rare Duesenberg 'J' Town Car Y-4d first issue in white with a red chassis and yellow roof and interior. These are highly sought after but very few have been found. Fakes exist, so caution is needed.

Over thirty different versions of the 1912 Rolls Royce Y-7c were made. It normally has dark red or black seats but two rare issues exist with either yellow or green seats.

The 1912 Ford Model T Van Y-13c can be found in many liveries. Arnott's Biscuits and Sunlight Soap are the most sought after.

The Sunbeam Motorcycle and Milford Sidecar Y-8b was a wonderful piece of engineering. The model always had a chrome-plated finish with a black saddle, and usually a dark green sidecar seat, but a few were issued with an emerald-green sidecar seat. These are quite rare but reproduction seats have been available for many years, so that there are many fakes around. Sunbeams were made in a variety of colours with a range of seat and saddle colours but these were not generally available to the public because they were made as trial pieces for the range's twenty-fifth anniversary.

In 1972 the 1938 Lagonda Drophead Coupe Y-11c was released. The first version has a gold-painted body but the wings and running boards can be painted purple, dark red, strawberry red or maroon. The maroon version is fairly common. The strawberry red and dark red are harder to find but the purple one is very rare. The Lagonda was later released in orange and gold, copper and gold, copper and black, cream and gold, and

Another 1912 Ford Model T, the Tanker Y-3d. It was released in several different liveries but the Zerolene version was a limited edition and so is quite hard to find.

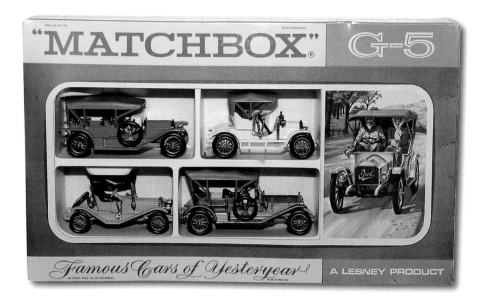

The Famous Cars of Yesteryear G-5 gift set. Unlike some of the '1-75' gift sets, no vehicles in the Models of Yesteryear sets were recoloured just for the sets, so these gift sets are relatively cheap and a good buy.

finally cream and black. The copper and gold is hard to find when it is fitted with green or red seats. The copper and black version is also hard to find, as is the cream and gold.

The 1930 Duesenberg 'J' Town Car Y-4d was first issued in 1976 and the first version was in white with a red chassis and yellow seats and hood. This model has gone on to become the firm favourite of Models of Yesteryear collectors because the seats and hood were quickly changed to black. Almost immediately the model was recoloured to dark red, so the white and red version with either the yellow seats or the black seats has become greatly sought after.

The very stately-looking 1912 Rolls Royce Y-7c was released in just three different colour schemes but with casting, plastic components and wheel variations this model has plenty to interest the Rolls Royce enthusiasts.

In 1979 the Ford Model T Van Y-12c made its first appearance, in the livery of Coca-Cola. The sides of the van were outlined with a red pinstripe. The second version had one of the vertical pinstripes removed from just in front of the rear wheels, so the van can be found with four or five vertical pinstripes. The four-line version is very common but the five-line version is rare. The van was recoloured many times and can be found in a number of liveries, which include Colman's Mustard, Suze, Smith's Crisps, Bird's Custard, Cerebos Salt, Arnott's Biscuits, Harrods, Sunlight Seife, Royal Mail, Captain Morgan, Hoover, Pepsi Cola, Motor 100, Imbach, Heinz and Rosella. In 1981 it was released in green, celebrating the twenty-fifth anniversary of the Models of Yesteryear range. The Sunlight version is fairly hard to find but the rest are very common owing to over-production.

In 1981 a second Ford Model T was released. This one was a Tanker , numbered Y-3d. It was also issued in a multitude of liveries, including BP, Express Dairy, Carnation, Red Crown, Shell, Mobiloil and Castrol. The 1981 Zerolene issue was a special limited edition and so is quite hard to find.

It is little known outside the specialist collecting community that from about 1975 onwards a few Lesney employees were producing special Yesteryear models specifically for the collectors' market. These were usually made in odd colours or with the wrong paint designs, displaying the wrong liveries or incorrectly coloured plastic components. These were shipped out of the factory on one of the staff double-decker buses, delivered to an east London toyshop and then sold to collectors. Today these models are sold as pre-production or colour-trial models but

This silver 1911 Daimler Y-13b (right) was especially made to commemorate Lesney's receipt of the Queen's Award for Industry in 1968. All Lesney employees were presented with one as a memento of this occasion.

A Models of Yesteryear Giftware cigarette box. Other companies tried to cash in on Lesney's success by marketing similar items using various Yesteryear models, so they can also be found inside paperweights, glass bottles and many other objects.

the majority are stolen items as Lesney was never paid for any of them. It all adds to the colourful history of Lesney.

One model that deserves special mention is the 1929 Scammell 100-ton Transporter Y-16e and its Great Eastern Railway locomotive load, not because it is a valuable rarity but because of its sheer magnificence. At 1 foot long (305 mm) it was the largest MoY model ever produced, and also the most expensive. In its day the transporter was the largest and most impressive vehicle on the road, though only two were ever made; it had a 7-litre four-cylinder engine and an eight-speed gearbox, but it had a top speed of only 6 mph and travelled a paltry 1 mile per gallon.

Yesteryear models were also used as part of Lesney's 'Giftware' range, for which selected models were chrome-plated or given a gold finish and mounted on ashtrays, wooden cigarette boxes, wooden pipe holders or, more usually, attached to china trays made by the Wade company. Although a rather specialised field of collecting, they can often be bought for very little outlay. Models of Yesteryear can also be found inserted into glass bottles or sealed inside Perspex paperweights made by Lesney or by other companies, but for these expect to pay a premium as they are eagerly sought by collectors.

SERVICE STATIONS, ROADWAYS AND CATALOGUES

T HE FIRST SERVICE Station MG-1 was released in 1957. At the time Lesney did not own any plastic-moulding equipment, so an outside contractor, Raphael Lipkin, was given the task. The single-storey building was moulded in red plastic and it had opening doors front and rear. Attached to the roof was a sign with a 'Matchbox Garage' label. The forecourt was moulded in yellow plastic and it had a space for the Esso Petrol Pumps set A-1.

Later, when Lesney obtained their own plastic-moulding equipment, they made their own Service Station to the same design, but the colours were reversed. This yellow building with red forecourt is slightly harder to find.

The second MG-1 Service Station came in 1961. It was a two-storey building moulded in red with a yellow forecourt and

The Service Stations MG-1a and MG-1b were supposedly based on a garage not far from the Lesney Eastway factory complex.

The recoloured BP Service Station, MG-1d. This was included with the BP Petrol Pumps and Sign and three '1-75' models in the G-10 gift set. This rare set was not in production for very long.

rear ramp. It was in the livery of Esso with a 'Matchbox Sales & Service Station' sign attached to the roof, and had a space for the Petrol Pump set A-1. In 1963 it was recoloured to white and green and the livery changed to BP. A new set of BP Petrol Pumps and Sign A-1 was made to accompany the garage.

In 1967 the third MG-1 BP Service Station was introduced. This one was a freestanding single-storey building moulded in white and it included a set of plastic pumps. Later a card forecourt was included in the set to add to play value, and later still a plastic service ramp became part of the set.

In 1971 a Superfast Auto Sales Lot was introduced. It was issued as part of the Accessory pack range and is quite hard to find. Several more garages were issued over the years but, being very toy-like, they hold little interest for collectors.

The Fire Station MF-1 appeared in 1963. It was normally moulded in red and white, or less commonly red and off-white, but early issues can be found with a green roof. The green roof is thought to have been moulded for an ambulance station that was never issued.

There was a series of Matchbox Roadways, numbered from R-1 to R-4, first introduced in 1960. Each comprised a

The Motorway Service Station MG-1f was released in 1971 with a plastic ramp and a card forecourt.

The Matchbox Roadway Layout R-2 'London' was a flat card layout.

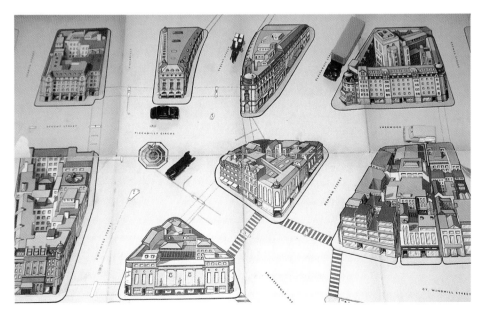

The Matchbox Fold Away Flyover R-1 was a later issue with a fold-out card roadside cafe, flyover and road signs.

Opposite: The Lap Counter SF-18 was only one of the many additions and attachments available to enhance the Superfast track.

fold-out card play mat printed with a selection of roadways. The first one was a simple flat play mat with roads and buildings printed in a three-dimensional style, but later ones had punch-out buildings that could be attached to the roadway. Probably the most attractive roadway was the Racetrack Speedway R-4, a racetrack with various punch-out stands, pits, stalls and signs.

Between 1960 and 1968 there were eleven roadways made in all. Some are fairly common but others can be extremely difficult to find.

The Matchbox Motorway was developed by the Arnold company in Germany. The first Lesney set was the M-1 Motorway, which was a simple oval of track for which a standard Matchbox car could be modified with nothing more than a plastic peg and sticker and driven round the

roadway using a hidden powered spring. It was quickly overtaken by the M-2 (or M-12), which was a figure of eight with a flyover. The E-1 was an extension kit to expand the set even further. Lesney made full use of television advertising to promote this product in time for Christmas 1968 and many sets were sold. But overloading the track with too many cars could stretch the springs and make it unusable,

The Matchbox Motorway was launched with the help of much television advertising.

A regular-wheel era catalogue (top) and a Superfast era catalogue (below). Pocket catalogues by their very nature are hard to find. There were also trade catalogues intended for retailers only, and these too are very hard to find.

and the springs did make a lot of noise when in use, so many Motorway sets did not get a great deal of use. Because of the large size of the set and the space that it takes up, they are not much sought by collectors. The sets contained two Matchbox models and sometimes they would include some very interesting and rare transitionals.

The Switchatrack, a figure-of-eight track with a central roundabout, made a brief appearance shortly after the Motorway but it was killed off by the rush to convert everything to Superfast wheels.

There was an attempt to reissue the Motorway as the M-400 in 1980 but the Superfast wheels tended to skid all over the road, and it could not have been very successful as it was deleted after only a year.

Hundreds of different Superfast track sets and various accessories were produced over the years as well as several Lanechanger track sets.

Matchbox pocket catalogues have always generated a great deal of interest among collectors, which no doubt is due to the sheer nostalgia that they can induce. Flicking through an old pocket catalogue can instantly bring back a flood of childhood memories.

The British pocket catalogues were first printed in 1957 but the earliest catalogues from the 1950s are virtually impossible to find. Those from the 1960s are available but

The Power Driver PD-1 was a single driven wheel that would also steer and could be attached to the base of a model. It could not have been very successful as they are rare nowadays.

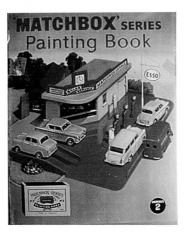

Matchbox Series Painting Books were made in the mid- to late 1950s and as they were designed to be painted very few of them have survived. A set of these in unused condition can easily be worth £1,000 or more.

Launched in 1973, the Matchbox 'Skybusters' was a series of eighteen aircraft ranging from the Pitts Special to the Space Shuttle. Each aircraft can be found in several different colours or liveries. Shown here is the Spitfire SB-8, the pride of the Royal Air Force.

take some hunting down. From the 1970s onwards they are widely available; by 1970 there were over 10 million catalogues being printed each year and so it is no surprise that the later issues are much easier to find.

Most British collectors are not aware that the catalogues were printed in a multitude of foreign languages, not just German, French and Italian, but Arabic and Japanese too. Add to those the many trade catalogues printed over the years and it is no wonder that this niche has such a strong following.

The Fire Station MF-1 was first made in 1963. It is shown with the Mercury Fire Chief 59d, Merryweather Fire Engine 35c and Land Rover Fire Truck 57c. In front are the Volkswagen 1600TL 67b and Ford Zodiac MkIV 53c.

THE FINAL DAYS

A FTER SEEING A constant growth in business, apart from during a brief period in 1969 following Mattel's introduction of Hot Wheels, Lesney was prospering, but, after they had purchased and rebuilt a couple of factories in the late 1970s and then bought out several other toy companies, the recession came and sales slumped. This caught Lesney unaware. They laid off staff and sold property, enabling them to struggle on until late 1982. Then the inevitable came and they ceased trading; the company was sold to Universal Toys of Hong Kong and our story comes to a close.

This book has traced the history of the diecast range of Lesney's Matchbox toys but the company also produced a great many plastic toys and model kits, which are beyond the remit of this book. The Matchbox brand-name lives on today, but under Mattel's ownership, and admittedly playing second fiddle to their Hot Wheels range of models. But Matchbox toys are still bringing delight to children everywhere, which is exactly what Sir Leslie Smith OBE and Sir Jack Odell OBE had intended.

FURTHER INFORMATION

BOOKS

Carbonel, Jean-Christophe. *1973–2010: The Story of Matchbox Kits*. Histoire & Collections, 2011.

Force, Edward. *Matchbox and Lledo Toys*. Schiffer Publishing, 1999.

Johnson, Dana. *Matchbox Toys 1947–2003*. Collector Books, 2008.

Larson, Tom. *Matchbox Field Guide*. Warman's Field Guides, 2008.

Mack, Charlie. *Collecting Matchbox Regular Wheels*. Schiffer Publishing, 2013. (USA price guide.)

Mack, Charlie. *Encyclopedia of Matchbox Toys*. Schiffer Publishing, 2013. (USA price guide.)

Macmullan, Kay. *The Collector's Corner*. Matchbox Toys, 2005.

McGimpsey, Kevin, and Orr, Stewart. *Collecting Matchbox Diecast Toys*. Major Productions, 1989.

McGimpsey, Kevin, and Orr, Stewart. *Matchbox – The Yesteryear Book*. Major Productions, 1996.

McGoldrick, Anthony A. *TV Toys*. Shire Library, 2013.

Ragan, Mac. *Matchbox Cars: The First 50 Years*. Motorbooks International, 2002.

Ramsay, John. *British Diecast Model Toy Catalogue*. Warners Group Publications, 2012. (UK price guide.)

Schiffer, Nancy. *Matchbox Toys*. Schiffer Publishing, 2003.

Scholl, Richard. *Matchbox Official 50th Anniversary*. Rizzoli International Publications, 2002.

Stonebeck, Bruce and Diane. *Matchbox Toys: A Collector's Guide*. Book Sales, 1993.

PERIODICALS

Collector's Gazette, Diecast Collector Magazine and *Model Collector Magazine* are all monthly publications that often have articles about Matchbox toys that will interest the collector. All three publications list auction details and have diaries that list the dates and venues of all toy fairs.

WEBSITES

www.vintagebritishdiecasts.co.uk Matchbox toys website. Information and price guides for most British-made diecasts.
www.matchboxmemories.com Models of Yesteryear website. Information on the Yesteryear range and Giftware.
www.fcarnahan.com Matchbox information, clubs and conventions (USA).
http://www.collectors-club-of-great-britain.co.uk/Events/Category/Toyfair--Swapmeet/_cat5 British toy fair calendar.

FORUMS

www.vintagebritishdiecasts.co.uk/forum/index.php Matchbox toys forum.
www.moyboyz.com/phpBB3 Models of Yesteryear forum.

PLACES TO VISIT

The following all have diecast models on display, though not necessarily Matchbox toys. Please check the opening times before travelling.
Bethnal Green Museum of Childhood, Cambridge Heath Road, London E2 9PA. Telephone: 020 8983 5200. www.museumofchildhood.org.uk
Bressingham Steam Experience, Low Road, Bressingham, Diss, Norfolk IP22 2AB. Telephone: 01379 686900. www.bressingham.co.uk

Cotswold Motoring Museum and Toy Collection, The
Old Mill, Bourton-on-the-Water, Gloucestershire
GL54 2BY. Telephone: 01451 821255.
www.cotswold-motor-museum.co.uk

Lakeland Motor Museum, Holker Hall and Gardens,
Cark-in-Cartmel, Grange-over-Sands, South Lakeland,
Cumbria LA11 7PL. Telephone: 01539 558509.
www.lakelandmotormuseum.co.uk

Museum of British Road Transport, Hales Street,
Coventry CV1 1PN. Telephone: 024 7623 4270.
www.transport-museum.com

National Motor Museum, John Montagu Building, Beaulieu,
Brockenhurst, Hampshire SO42 7ZN. Telephone: 01590
612345. www.beaulieu.co.uk

Romney, Hythe and Dymchurch Toy and Model Museum,
New Romney Station, New Romney, Kent TN28 8PL.
Telephone: 01797 362353. www.rhdr.org.uk

West Wales Museum of Childhood, Pen-Ffynnon, Llangeler,
Carmarthenshire SA44 5EY. Telephone: 01559 370428.
www.toymuseumwales.co.uk

COLLECTORS' CLUBS

Coventry Diecast Model Club. Contact: Hugh Evans.
Telephone: 023 7641 9124.

East Anglian Model Club. PO Box 60, Norwich NR4 7WB.
Email: jnking@ukonline.co.uk

Maidenhead Static Model Club. Contact: Michael Forbes.
Telephone: 01933 665569.

Wessex Toy and Model Club. Contact: Doug Male.
Telephone: 01225 755043.

INDEX